5/19/24

You can honestly write about grief if you've been there. Jonathan *has* been there and still carries its presence. Yes, this beautiful little book is about grief, but even more about life. I wept my way through it, and with every page, I knew ... I love, love, love this book.

—PAUL YOUNG, author of *The Shack*

Exquisitely etched, in a luring cadence, a daughter lost, a family fractured, fractioned, all in the lower case, not shouting at us, but hard to read. I had to stop and regain my composure. What is this terrible beauty? Not a theology but something softer, more delicate, unprotected, exposed. What is this? A moving poem, certainly, but also a prayer, a wounded word, a broken hallelujah, where a random hug, a hand held through the night, a shoulder touched, are the only amelioration, the only God worthy of our time, the only God there may be, the only way to keep the future open.

—JOHN CAPUTO, Thomas J. Watson Professor Emeritus of Religion, Syracuse University and David R. Cook Professor Emeritus of Philosophy Villanova University, author of *The Insistence of God: A Theology of Perhaps*

The dark beauty of grief working as art glows through every stanza of this long, slender epic. In the gripping insistence of its poetic cadences, it extends a shadowed comfort, suspensefully unfolding, for losses already or yet to be suffered. Its meditative revelation forces no belief, no solution—it invites only honesty, possibility, creativity.

—CATHERINE KELLER, George T. Cobb Professor of Constructive Theology, Drew University Theological School, author of *Facing Apocalypse: Climate, Democracy and Other Last Chances*.

When it comes to loss, the philosophical 'problem of pain' becomes the unbearable mystery of suffering. This is the state in which we are lost in an endless sea of misery, and where we must attempt to survive through the process of mourning. With *indigo*, Jonathan Foster invites the reader into his encounter with grief. In this stunning reflection on loss and suffering, we do not simply observe one person's grief but find words that might help us as we tarry with our own.

—PETER ROLLINS, author of *The Idolatry of God: Breaking Our Addiction to Certainty and Satisfaction*

The words are exquisite poetry. The narrative style, unique. The pain is both universal and particular to the circumstances of Jonathan's one-of-a-kind life. The hope *indigo* offers is unconventional and yet genuine. I felt this book. I hope you pick a copy up and feel it too.

—**THOMAS JAY OORD**, author of *God Can't: How to Believe in God and Love after Tragedy, Abuse, and Other Evils*

This text ranks with C.S. Lewis's *A Grief Observed* in its description of grief from the inside, the never-ending healing process, the thoughtless comments of religious people, and the reality that even when life becomes full again, the emptiness remains. We mourn and yet we are grateful for all that has been and hopeful of what will come in claiming the joy and sorrow of life.

—**BRUCE EPPERLY**, author of *The Elephant is Running: Process and Open and Relational Theologies and Religious Pluralism*

I wasn't ready for this book. Write me an essay, and I'll play with it, argue with it, even try to pick it apart. Write me something artful, and I am defenseless. I think they call it *aesthetic arrest*, the way I cried and laughed my way through this piece of writing—so beautiful and sad, so funny, raw and insightful that I literally couldn't put it down. I haven't faced all Jonathan Foster has faced, but I have known grief, the confusion of parenting, the sting of regret, the madness of sorrow so relentlessly exploding its "little detonations of sadness" into my ordinary days. *indigo* has reminded me that I must choose to remain present to my own life, to be unguarded and let the world get to me—the joy and the pain of it all—with a tender heart and thick skin, and it almost makes me believe I can do it. I'm grateful for my encounter with *indigo*. I hope you'll encounter it, too.

—**TIM SUTTLE**, author of *Shrink: Faithful Ministry in a Church-Growth Culture* and Sr Pastor of Redemption Church

This book is absolutely stunning. Jonathan has written on grief in a way that only someone interacting with it can—someone who has wrestled with it, been smothered by it, and has (in some strangely beautiful way) befriended it. If loss has come beating on the doors of your life, making an un-welcomed appearance, this book is for you, for in it you will find a friend who will help you access tears that might be stuck and then wipe those tears from your eyes as you search for the courage to take a step forward into whatever tomorrow might hold.

—GLENN SIEPERT, host of the *What If Project* podcast, author of *Emerging from the Rubble*

Shortly into this book, I realized I was reading something sacred. It caught me off guard and beckoned me to pay attention. Wherever you find yourself, I'm confident *indigo* will invite you into the holy ground of ashes and beauty. This book is a gift.

—HEATHER HAMILTON, author of *Returning to Eden: A Field Guide for the Spiritual Journey*

indigo is an understated masterpiece that makes audible an astonishing voice of heartful experience and profound wisdom, not a voice asking us to redeem the everyday by recourse to one or another distant infinity, but rather to realize—if only in remembering what now is lost to us—how the everyday IS the infinite.

—RICHARD BOOTHBY, author of *Blown Away: Refinding Life After My Son's Suicide*

Reading this poignant and profound book took me deep into an *indigo* presence of both life/beauty and death/loss. If you're considering loss you'll be grateful for this book ... which is simultaneously heart-breaking, heart-opening, and heart-expanding.

—BRIAN D. MCLAREN, author of *Faith After Doubt*

indigo
the color of grief

jonathan j. foster

Copyright © 2023 by Jonathan J. Foster
Formatting: Nicole Jones Sturk
Cover graphic and design: Jonathan Foster
Editing: editorialdepartment.com

All rights reserved. This book or any portion thereof may not be reproduced or used in any manner whatsoever without the express written permission of the publisher except for the use of brief quotations in a book review or scholarly journal.

NO AI TRAINING: Without in any way limiting the author [and publisher's] exclusive rights under copyright, any use of this publication to "train" generative artificial intelligence (AI) technologies to generate text is expressly prohibited. The author reserves all rights to license uses of this work for generative AI training and development of machine learning language models.

Print ISBN: 978-1-7376649-6-3
Ebook ISBN: 978-1-7376649-5-6

Printed in the United States of America Library of Congress Cataloguing-in-Publication Data
indigo: the color of grief / Jonathan J. Foster

What most profoundly sets speech in motion
is a dimension of absence in perception,
a lack that haunts perceptual presence,
a dimension of perception
that remains unrecognizable.

Richard Boothby

If there is a post-Anthropocene
worth living in
those who will live in it
will need different stories.

Isabelle Stengers

Knowledge will come to an end;
love never ends.

Paul

contents

preface 1

prologue: thunder. 5
absence. 9
loved 11
4/5s 17
early 25
midday. 29
late 33
interpretation. 39
love 43
shocking. 47
weeks 51
beauty 55
music 59
listening. 63
she's 65
followed. 73
anyone 79
strange 87
friendship. 89

solidarity 93

hugs 99

retraced 103

heaven 111

moms 117

grieving 125

home 129

and 135

epilogue: present 137

endnotes 141

acknowledgments 145

about the author 147

preface

i have written this story
the way i received it
the way it's been bouncing
around inside
        conversational tone
        short sentences
        hints
        suspicions
        little punctuation
        no capitalization

idk all the reasons why

        maybe i like the idea of a
        lowercase theology
        something that doesn't
        SHOUT

        maybe space on the page
        will encourage you
        to explore what's going on in your   space

        maybe loss has left me
        feeling out of control
        and making up my own
        rules is me taking control back

      maybe it's just about grammar
      honestly i was going to mess
      a bnch of it up anyhow

whatever the reason
it's here now ... with you

i hope you'll take a breath
and be here ... with it

prologue

thunder
and brooding skies
sent us scrambling down
the mountainside

shale and rock
went before us
rain came behind us and
then on top of us
      little explosions of
      rocky mountain
      raindrops
      dramatically bursting
      on shoulders and heads
      amplified by
      plastic-hooded raincoats

we ducked
below the tree line
and found an outcrop
of rock and root
just big enough for
father and i to fit
within and
underneath

i remember
smell of atmosphere
sway of pine trees
buzz of charged air
the sense of a terrible beauty

and then
a single
bolt of lightning

it was a brilliant detonation
across the backdrop of
all i could see

it flashed
in an instant
though for a second or
two i could see the outline
of its power etched
in the air
lingering

    electricity
    of the past
    throbbing beauty
    of the present

----

my daughter was a
twenty-year lightning strike
brilliant detonation

across the backdrop of
all we were

she flashed
in what now
seems like an
instant

though i think i
still see the outline
of her power
etched into the air
lingering

        electricity
        of the past
        throbbing beauty
        of the present

absence
is protagonist now

it's weird
absence is nothing
a no-thing
but it's very much something
a some-thing

it has no form but
it forms me
it has no energy but
it energizes me
i'm full of its emptiness

only now occurs to me
(ninety-nine months beyond
daughter of lightning
flash of car wreck)
that all these words
might be an attempt to
absorb the shock
control the effect
fill the emptiness

as if the thing-ness of words
can fill this wordless no-thing

      i have an image of
      youngest son

maybe age five
poolside
struggling to get a toy
out of his pocket

he's wrestling wet shorts
hands reaching
turning round and round

i watch him for a
whole hour one minute
as he spins
never getting anywhere

a boy chasing an object
like a dog chasing a tail
a world chasing a sun
a sun chasing a galaxy
a galaxy chasing a cosmos

that's me
trying to trap
questions with my creeds
shadows with my candles
lightning with my eyes

that's me
trying to address
the no-thing
with me
always

loved
being a dad
loved being *her* dad

      bedtime prayers
      shoulder growing damp
      her hair wet from evening bath
      making up jokes
      songs

      choir concerts
      shafts of light
      high school auditorium
      smiling shoulder touching
      wife's shoulder smiling

      staying late after
      soccer practice
      teammates waving
      her and i kicking the ball
      lights going out
      one
      by
      one
      taco-bell drive thru on the way
      home

i'd do some things differently
but thankfully there are

few regrets
though i have one for sure
    she was about 10 (mid-life)
    at a soccer tournament
    four games over the
    weekend
    each played with less
    desire
    than the one before

    with other girls
    heading to cars
    sucking on orange slices
    receiving accolades from grandparents
    who had flown
    all the way from
    minnesota
    to see such terrific soccer
    my daughter
    followed my pointing finger
    back out onto the field

    she kicked
    dribbled
    and ran with me
    and all the
    expectations

    i imagine
    more than a few parents
    exchanged glances
    as they quickly exited the parking lot
    trying to minimize possibility

of their daughters witnessing
such wild parenting

i don't blame them
it was probably too much

on the way home
i looked in the
rearview mirror
and saw a little cloud
of sadness pass across
my girl's countenance

broke my heart a bit, said
> *hey*
> *babe*
> *that was too much*
> *i'm so sorry*

she snatched a tear, said
> *it's okay dad*
> *i know you're just trying to*
> *make me better*

good grief
a 10-year-old isn't
supposed
to be so patient
didn't know whether
to laugh or cry

still don't

during middle school years
i'd find her in her room
busy with
homework
journal
music

i'd bump her pencil
jab her arm
toss a pillow
at her

usually morphed
into a game
we'd see
who
could push
who
off the bed
usually ended same way
    crooked lampshade
    laughter
    me on the floor
    her jumping on top of me

sometimes she wasn't into it
(hard to imagine)
she'd tolerate it
for a minute then
tell me to leave

then i'd have to
find her brothers
and mess with them

most of my
parenting approach
was to annoy the kids
until they started
wrestling with me

if i was a neurologist
i'd probably write about
neurochemicals
the way they're released
when we physically interact with
loved ones

i've loved being a dad

lots of neurochemicals

4/5s
became
the reality
in the span of a
heartbeat

her heart
stopped beating
in a span of a
heartbeat
and we were 4/5s
        a fraction

a fraction
doesn't work
like a whole
~~something~~
someone
is missing

it's more than
just someone missing
it's also the role
the someone played

her role in our family
was something like
a catalyst or
initiator

we didn't assign
the role it's just
who she was from
day one

more wind
than weathervane
more thermostat
than thermometer

like, if the boys
were mired in a mood
she could pull them out
but flip the script and
boys had little chance

she was her own
strong
intentional
capable
person

    remember being with
    extended family once
    when great grandmother fainted
    and passed out for a moment

    she recovered quickly
    but for a few minutes
    we were unsure of
    how it would turn out

several of the
pre-teenaged cousins
ran to the basement
upset about the event
but even more upset about
our girl not showing
enough emotion regarding possibility
that great grandmother might
no longer be alive

their concerns escalated
in volume and intensity
until finally
our girl stood up
with fists pointed to the ground
and announced to the whole group
> *look*
> *i'll cry*
> *once we find out grandma*
> *is actually dead*

the room calmed

apparently
the cousins thought
the logic was sound

yeah, she could change
the environment
when she wanted

this was what
we were used to
she was a force of life
that could initiate
and shape life
in others
    cousins
    brothers
    friends
    wife
    me

and then?
the force
was gone

she died
and certain
parts of us died
[ ]

    remember the first real trip
    we made as a fraction
        "family" vacation
        playing board games
        so awkward
        at some point during the evening
        i sat back and watched
        the four of us
        doing our best
        learning how to interact
        without her
            less neurochemicals

less laughter
less volume too

an image
materialized
in my mind's eye

something revealing
neurological activity
within a group of people

yeah, some kind of
visual spectrometer kind of thing
displaying the interaction
bouncing around
within a family of five doing life
    you know, interacting
    playing
    arguing
    talking
    singing
    taking trips together

    with her: a range of colors
    burst across the display
    without her: areas
    noticeably muted

    more than that
    there were specific areas of
    the visual projection
    the thing displaying
    the interaction

        bouncing around
        within a family of five doing life
            you know, interacting
            playing
            arguing
            talking
            singing
            taking trips together
    that were completely dark

that night
after the board games
after the visual spectrometer kind of thing
yeah, that night
was the worst

couldn't relax
couldn't sleep
rotating ceiling fan
slowly
shadow of cloud and moon

i'd get up and go somewhere
but there was no place to go
to get away from my thoughts
to get away from me
to get away

kept thinking about
the way she could light
brothers up
kept thinking about
their neurological activity

changed forever
marriage changed forever
me changed

forever

kept seeing dark spots on
that stupid visual display
fuckin interactive visual spectrometer-thing
kept apologizing to whoever was listening
for saying *fuck*

just kept thinking about
how much fun it all
used to be
before the day
everything
changed

early

new year's day
the sun rose
> though the sky
> barely noticed
> draped as it was
> in gray the
> color of wet tweed

i stood at
the picture window
mother-in-love's house
hilltop
overlooking
the road that descended
down and through barns
various shades of white
each one fading further into the mist

i sat
and read elie wiesel's
iconic book *night*
(in the morning i read *night*)

i alternated
between reading passages
and looking out picture window

between shadowy edge
of what i could understand
        scapegoating
        nazis
        violence
        dullness of war
        hung up on barbed wire fences

and the fogged-in edge
of all i could see
        trees
        like fingers
        down by the river
        reaching up
        to find the light

wiesel's *night*
is a work of art
stunning
if not sickening

one story in particular
materialized in my mind's eye
        the entire camp
        made to march
        underneath three young
        jewish men
        hanging

        wiesel writes about hearing
        a voice cry out

as he passes underneath, said
where is God?

then another voice, said
*where is God? he is hanging there
on the gallows with those boys*

i closed
the book softly
reverently
and exhaled

tried to imagine
absurdity of such violence
tried to imagine
the beauty of wiesel's writing
amid absurdity of such violence

didn't reopen the book that day

idk
seemed disrespectful
to move on too quickly
to read further
to possibly forget
what wiesel wanted us to remember

so that call and response …
where is God?

*where is God? he is hanging there
on the gallows with those boys*
stuck with me

throughout the day
it bounced around
in caves
somewhere inside
muted for a while
then reappeared

wasn't trying to think about it
wasn't trying *not* to think about it
it just kept echoing
      making the bed
      cleaning the dishes
      walking the dog …
           where is God?

           where is God? he is hanging there
           on the gallows with those boys

midday
activities revolved around
our girl preparing to leave

she was traveling
to meet her friend's family
a boy

it was her first trip
like this
travelling
to meet her friend's family
a boy

she packed bags
loaded the car
said goodbye

a couple of times

she was eager to leave
but wasn't leaving
she walked by
another time or two
before i recognized
she was probably anxious

it was sweet or
cute or
fun?

yeah, i think fun
is the word
like, it's really fun to be a parent
and experience
your kid experience
something new

i nodded her direction, said
    are you nervous?

her eyes burnished
blue and deep
reminiscent
of first time i saw her

        birthing room
        baby warming oven thing

        i left her mom's side
        and walked over
        to meet her
        huge coal for eyes
        searching
        blinking
        slow-motion
        tractor beam
        pulling me in
        my heart thumping
        or breaking
        in love

        i was twenty-six
        healthy

confident
and had no idea
until she looked at me
how vulnerable i was

within a few days
her eyes
transitioned into
something blue
something for which i had
no name
though
in recent years
i've been thinking the blue
as undomesticated and marine

her life too

yeah, storms of wildness
oceanic shades
of laughter
stormy depths
of brooding

she was exhausting and fun
twain wrote about his daughter, said
> *she was a magazine of feelings*
> *and they were of all kinds and shades of force*
> *and she was so volatile as a little child*
> *that sometimes the whole battery*
> *came into play in the short compass of a day*
> *joy, sorrow, anger, remorse,*

storm, sunshine, rain, darkness
they were all there
they came in a moment
and they were gone as quickly

sounds about right

so i caught her eye, said
    are you nervous?

   yes
she laughed
    i'm nervous

we hugged again
and
then
she
left

late
new year's day afternoon
about the time
we expected the phone to ring
it didn't

phones not ringing
make parents un
easy

we logged onto
a few sites
made a
few calls
realized the weather
where she was headed
had turned
icy

the house throbbed
with anxiety

i was back at
picture window
pacing

searching
for signs

anything
that might bring news
about car wrecks
about ice storms
about survivors
of car wrecks
in ice storms

down by the river
trees like fingers
reached to grab the last
horizontal slice of
burnt
orange
indigo
as everything faded to
black

headlights turned
off the highway
turned past an empty field
dotted with a few shivering
cornstalks

> stomach turned too
> hope and fear
>
> was like pushing
> brake pedal and gas pedal
> at the same time
>
> i longed to hear news about
> my daughter

but i knew highway patrolmen
do not stop
by farmhouses
at sunsets
on new year's days
to bring good news

headlights bounced
across cattle grate
bounced across
cows
refulgent
wide-eyed
trying to get out of the way

headlights grew stronger
up the hill
lost for a moment
in darkness

then straight at
farmhouse
straight at
picture window
straight at
me
bowed
head

highway patrolman
stepped inside
with his back against

the wall
he faced us

he gripped
and regripped
the edge of his hat
that slowly turned
as he spoke in
soft
short
controlled
khaki
sentences

then he took
the slightest step
backwards
i think
to create space
to soften the blow

    bless the people who
    do these things
    try and create space
    try and soften the blow
    be the first to let a family
    know
    it's forever a
    fraction

he paused, said
    she didn't make it

and then
everything is breaking open
pain calling to pain
deep calling to deep
[ ]

after some time passed
idk how much time
because
it's all jumbled
up for a bit

like, the system has glitched
and i'm seeing her
in pixelated cracks of
light
hearing her
in distorted patches of
audio

and simultaneously
seeing
hearing
my family all around me
     4/5s

but after some time passed
idk how much time
because
it's all jumbled
up for a bit

audio
in distorted patches of
hearing her
light
in pixelated cracks
and i'm seeing her
like, the system has glitched
[ ]

after some time passed
i leaned up against
something
and craziest thing
that call and response
i had been hearing all day …
    where is God?

    where is God? he is hanging there
    on the gallows with those boys

i heard it again
except this time
i heard …
    where was God?

    where was God? he was in that car
    dying with quincy

interpretation
of such ridiculous news
offered up by voices
in one's head
during times of duress
should probably
be avoided

honestly
i should
be silent
be still
let it
be

but i can't resist

idk why

maybe fear
fear the whole thing will be
co-opted by
special interest groups

or maybe it's a natural response
like rubbing your shoulder
after running into a doorway or something
(this the most severe of doorways)

maybe i feel
responsibility
as a dad
human
future ancestor
to be present to this thing
to figure it out

maybe it's arrogance

maybe all the above

whatever the motivation
i heard something
and though the sound i heard
this voice
that elie wiesel introduced to me
this, this … *thing*
that emerged in my life
or out of my life
from his story
to my story
now into *your* story

gave no details about
what it means when
Gods are dying with
young people
on gallows
and in car wrecks

gave no details about
what comes next

like, if hope wins
or if we're all just fingers reaching
to grab the last horizontal slice of
burnt
orange
indigo
as everything fades to
black

gave no details about *anything*
other than
God being
present to us
in death

what's not lost on me is
there *was* a voice

could it have been a voice
placed there by wiesel's story?
like, could his story about God
with those boys
in death
have primed me to imagine God
with my daughter
in death?

      yes, i think so

could it have been
a kind of
neurological hallucination?

yes, i think so

could it have been
an expression
of love?

yes, i think so

love
is probably talked
about too much
and not enough

i suspect love wins
(who would i be
if i didn't admit such suspicions?)
but i also suspect "wins"
isn't exactly the word
given the way it signifies
completeness or
autonomy or
wholeness or
things impervious to loss
(what would love be without loss?)

i think love's victory
is in its fierce capacity
to endure during
great resistance

endurance
is patience
and patience
is love

love is terrible
because the increase

of its capacity
is forever tied to resistance
        a thousand different ways
        hope is deferred
                divorce
                disease
                denial
                danger
                debt
                deceit
                disgrace
                death

i have known resistance
been flattened
by wind and howl
worst of my fears
thinking
        life is over
        everything is over
        nothing matters

but also thinking
        wait, what is this which
        i am flattened against?

~~is it possible?~~
i think it's possible
that something or
someone is
the thing against
which i am flattened

the thing
holding things
together

idk
if it's love
but i want it to be
and if it's true
oh God, just think if it's true …

if it's true
there's hope

shocking
to lose something
so important

i mean, this wasn't like
the remote or
keys or
even a
famous painting

this was something actually priceless

how could this
happen?
how could someone
so full of life
lose their kid?

how could a kid
so full of life
be gone?

couldn't wrap
my mind
around
her departure

       in the dead of winter
       age 20
       threshold of adulthood

threshold of next
not unlike a spring season
for her
so she died
full of life and spring
in the dead of winter?
       what the…?

she had so much life to live
       wait… what was the point?

we had been getting her to
adulthood
showing her how
leading the way
    shoe-tying
    piano-playing
    stick-shift driving
a thousand things
    we did it
    she observed
    then followed

that's the way this works
kids follow parents
but then she died
and the sequence
was wrecked

hurt so bad

messed up eating
messed up sleeping

messed up eliminating waste
messed up routine
messed up directions to post office

messed up everything

i'd be talking
and words would start acting
like little tripwires
connected to
little memories
connected to
little detonations
of sadness

just normal conversations
        dentist or
        barber or
        grocery store
                have any kids?
                sons?
                daughters?
                how many kids do you have?

next thing i knew
i was slipping behind closed doors
trying not to make a scene
in public space
        dentist or
        barber or
        grocery store

yeah, just trying to find
secluded place to
make room for
little detonations
of sadness

weeks
until the headstone arrived
until the sunshine arrived
march maybe
maybe april
little flames of sprouting green
all throughout the cemetery
in springtime

in springtime
we went to see the grave marker
to mark her grave with flowers
wife and me

i'll not soon forget intentional
    way she knelt
    took a breath
    and arranged
    uprooted plants

    way she leaned
    back on heels
    fingers absently gripping
    fistfuls of grass

    way she snatched a tear with
    the back of her hand
    dirt and moisture creating
    little patterns of grief
    on her cheek

way her hair fell
over her face
way i felt looking at her
how much i loved her
how much i wanted to
throw up

i stood close
~~like a tree providing shade~~
~~like a sentinel providing protection~~
useless

she arranged and then rearranged
as if this spot
might be fixed
with uprooted plants
as if uprooted lives
might be fixed
with an arrangement of
uprooted plants

started to say
it doesn't matter

started to say
nothing matters

but i stopped
because something
very much started to matter
in the way she worked
so diligently amid
the sadness

i've thought
five or
thirty-seven or
a thousand times since

> *what is life*
> *if not beauty's pursuit*
> *at the edge of the grave?*

beauty
is a harmony
within
a melody
within
a key
signatured
by resistance

beauty isn't the
domination of
resistance
beauty is a type
of defiance
in the midst of
resistance

beauty is found
in the overlap

overlap isn't static
overlap is
fluid
responsive
movement

beauty
is constantly passing
away but also
the hope of the world

for in its passing
we find
an impression
      wound
      arrow
      symbol
pointing
to the possibility of
more

i'm guessing beauty is
always looking to
dialogue with us
though i'm not sure
we're always looking to
dialogue with beauty
there's just
so
much
damn
monologue

monologue
has never really been
that interested in beauty

beauty is
shy
invitational
luring
erotic

lives in
curves more than
corners
whispers more than
shouts
delay more than
dispatch

morality serves a purpose
knowledge does its thing
and truth is important
but in the end
(and all the endings after that)
beauty is the longing

i have lived this way for
quite some time
but it's only been
in recent years
living as i have with
so much absence
that i've gained
the language or
confidence or
arrogance
to offer my suspicions publicly

which is to say
beauty is truth
more than
truth is truth

music
was a big part
of our girl's life
>	church
>	school
>	in the car
>	with brothers

i suppose
there's nothing
i miss more
than hearing her
and the boys
sing random songs
in the living room

having kids
harmonize
is the best

music was
a refuge
a way to interact
with all the stuff
she was feeling
a way to process life

not hearing her sing
is painful

hearing so much silence
is deafening

i've scrolled through her phone
searching for recordings
flipped through her notebooks
looking for lyrics
just trying to find something
to recapture the music
but it never quite works

the music i have found
the songs she has finished is
comforting
but the music she didn't finish
     recordings that stop awkwardly
     lyrics that trail off at end of page
          yeah, none of that is comforting

and then i spend
rest of the day
wondering what line
she would have written next
to finish the song
and whatever sense of gratitude
i have about her music
is overwhelmed by
the sense of pain
i have about her unfinished music

and then i spend
rest of the week
wondering what

she would have done in her life
and whatever sense of gratitude
i have about
the person she was
is overwhelmed by
the sense of pain
i have about
the person she was *becoming*

    she was an unfinished song

sometimes
when people are over
and she and the boys
aren't singing
i want to raise my hands
quiet the room and say
    wait
    can you hear that?
    can you hear the music not playing?

listening

to music
that's not playing
is weird

she isn't singing
but the space she
used to occupy has
its own kind of sound

        remember learning about
        negative space
        which is an approach
        to art that interacts with
        the emptiness in background

        the role it plays
        the way it shares an
        e   with a subject in a
        d   painting
        g   photograph
        e   design

        the emptiness
        might be an
        imprint or outline
        a trace or track
        but it's presence
        is not incidental

reflect upon a piece of art
incorporating negative space
long enough
and you realize
extra stuff is going on

after a while
you think
> *maybe the subject*
> *isn't the subject*
> *without the empty part*

a while longer
you think
> *maybe the subject*
> *is the empty part*

about three days later
you think
> *wait*
> *maybe empty parts aren't empty*

        sounds about right

she's
been removed
by the event
but something's there
in the *eventing*

eventing is
living in the
wake of the event

like humans
on side of mountain
in the wake of colossal storm

more than
storm itself
this *eventing* is
depth of silence
on back end of such
an ungovernable force

it's
the smallness
after
the bigness

it's the
stunning realization
of how utterly wild
everything can be

stunning realization
of how utterly wild
everything *actually is*

eventing is grieving

grieving is never clearly
defined
named
closed
put away or
separated from everything else

grieving is
mountainrainthunderskybrilliancestormhumansterriblehope
       entanglement

grieving isn't something
to be ignored
so one can get on
with the living

rather
grieving is the wrenching
between thing gone
       person
       idea
       dream
       relationship
       hope
       life

and new thing longing to arrive
    person
    idea
    dream
    relationship
    hope
    life

grieving is
death
decay
compost
brilliant
irreparable
resignation
and also
emergence

grieving is procreative
grieving is living

blessed are those
interested in living

grieving
is an honest living
blessed are those
interested in honesty

more than truth-telling
honesty might be
a kind of
internal structural integrity

owning the sadness
isn't a sign
of weakness
it's a sign of
internal structural integrity

not saying this is
exactly how all this
must be done but i've
never been interested in
separating
grief from life

never been interested in
bottling sadness
like bottling peaches
to store in the basement
to be retrieved
from time to time
when one is ready to
consume peaches
when the peaches
are ready to be consumed

doing that
like, denying the sadness?
doesn't feel genuine
plus
seems like i'd do irreparable
damage to my insides
my spleen or something
      holding all that inside

so i do my best to
slip behind closed doors
you know, try not to make a scene
in public spaces

but i do not
back down
from grieving

again
not saying
what anyone else has to do
not trying to make others
feel bad about
not grieving or
not showing emotion or
not using words that
so easily
trip little detonations of sadness
because honestly
i think everyone's
just got to figure out their
own way

no, i'm not interested in shaming
only to give you freedom
from anyone or anything
possibly shaming you
about grieving
and also
to say that if you
identify as male

that you likely
suck at this

whether you
do grieving
in public or private
idk
i only know
you must learn how
to allow
the sadness

    remember watching the movie
    wind river

    the show plays out
    against the backdrop of
    wyoming
    wilderness
    fatherhood

    the main character
    familiar with loss
    finds his friend martin
    who just lost a daughter, says
        i'd like to tell you it gets easier
        but it doesn't
        if there's any comfort
        it's getting used to the pain
        i suppose

        i went to a grief seminar in casper
        did you know that?

followed

oldest son upstairs
night after his sister died

at the top step he
turned
put his hand up
stopping me
stopping the reality
stopping all the sadness
    dad
    wait
    i can't do this
    this hurts too much

i exhaled
my heart
an anvil

the whole thing
so unfair
for my daughter
for my son(s)
though idk what to think
about fairness

    idk what to think
    about the person born with
    impaired vision
    who can now see

because they have a part of my
daughter's eyes
cornea, i think
the part that helps refract light
[ ]

whatever the
hell fairness is
this was unfair
for my son
and the hurt was unlike
anything i had ever felt

no one tells you this
and even if they did
you wouldn't understand
but when you become a parent
something happens to all your
internal settings

like, all the dials and switches
you've dialed and switched
throughout your whole life
to protect your heart
to regulate your emotions
to monitor your empathy
they get all messed up

all of a sudden
you're this highly
empathic
compassionate
touchy feely

person
(at least when it
comes to your child)

yeah, parents with
hurting children
can easily un
hinge

next time you're at a
soccer game
cheer tryout
family get together
and some parent
starts getting weird
don't get overly judgmental

i mean
set some boundaries
if you need to
but good grief
these poor people
have had
all their internal
dials and switches
messed up

    remember sitting in the stands
    at son's basketball game once
    small gym
    which meant parents
    from both teams
    had to sit close together

seating arrangement
was me
right next to
a parent from our team
right next to
a parent from other team

parent from other team
was obnoxious
yelling
at refs
about our players
finally parent from our team
had enough, said
> *hey, can you please not*
> *be such a jerk and yell*
> *at our boys?*

parent from other team
shot back
> *i'm just keeping it real*

parent from our team
got in their face, said
> *well in that case*
> *your teeth are crooked*

classic

yeah, when
you're a parent
you feel deeply

about anything
dealing with
your offspring
and a parent who has
lost one of their children
grieves the loss
multiple times over
in multiple ways and
never more so
than when they grieve
what their living children have
lost

watching your kid
bear the loss
of their best friend
is unbearable

so, i cobbled
a response
together
for my son
that night
in the half-light
of the stairway
half-dark of fairness

best i could do
under the circumstances
though now i'm thinking
it works under any circumstance

it's probably
third or fourth best thing
i've ever come up with, said
> maybe there's so much pain here
> because there is so much love
>
> some people don't get to experience
> this kind of pain
> maybe in this way
> the pain is something for which to be
> thankful

anyone
who's ever mourned anything
has a story about well-intentioned
people saying dumb things

    once, after murder
        sitting in restaurant
        with clergy person
        (my boss at the time)
        i think he'd already ordered
        think he was waiting on me
        to decide what i wanted to eat

            remember looking at a swan
            outside the window
            in arizona
            stunning winter day
            in arizona
            sun
            perfect weight of a blanket
            draped over everything

            my eyes saw all that
            but my brain saw my sister
            lying awkwardly in a frozen ditch
            in iowa
            clothes ripped
            no blanket of sun
            stunning winter night in iowa

couldn't figure out
what i wanted for lunch
after a bit
i gathered he was
impatient for me to order
impatient for me to get over
whatever it was i wasn't getting over

watched me, then said
>   *we don't need to use*
>   *an event as a crutch*

i didn't think that was helpful
suggested as much
he rolled his eyes, quipped
>   *you know*
>   *it's always something*

once, after house burning
>   remember smoke drifting
>   up and down neighborhood
>   remember my wife standing on street
>   in front of the house
>   in front of what was *left* of the house
>   hand slowly rubbing forehead
>   trying to help brain process
>   the fire roaring
>   at the intersection of
>   two giant talismans of water
>   where kitchen once met kid's bedroom

acquaintance tapped my shoulder
yelled over the commotion, said

it's good this is happening to you
rather than someone without faith

once, after a friend from college died unexpectedly
    remember going to see his wife
    pregnant widow
    with two little boys
    some hugs and tears
    and then she left the room

    she returned with
    a funny smile and a gift
    turns out
    my friend had bought something
    for me
    the day before he died
        double box of cap'n crunch with cd-rom
        inside

    that's the kind of friend he was
    posthumously giving away
    double boxes of cap'n crunch with cd-roms inside

    dumbest best gift i ever received
        joni mitchell
        could have been singing
        about my friend, said
            don't it always seem to go
            that you don't know what you've got
            til it's gone

    and at the funeral
    acquaintance found me, said

God must have needed him there
more than we needed him here

once, about a year following
my daughter's death
religious acquaintance found me
following a worship service
to speak truth in love
to get to the heart of the matter
you know, have a real
"iron sharpening iron" moment, said
> *i don't think you want to feel better*
> *you know what?*
eyes narrowing
> *i challenge you*
> *to listen to christian radio*
> *nothing else*
> *for 90 days*

i smiled awkwardly, said
> nothing
> stood there as they
> walked away
> thinking how awful
> it would be
> to listen to christian radio
> nothing else
> for 90 days

once
actually, just about every time
i've experienced

something challenging
someone has said
> *everything happens for a reason*

(palm to face)
i have come to loathe this saying
i know religion world
is trying to help us cope

they mean well
but think about it
if everything happens for a reason
then what is the point of
anything?

why tell a battered partner to
leave a relationship?
why struggle to help those
flattened by injustice?
why work to highlight the
plight of the victim?

if everything happens
for a reason
one shouldn't get involved
for fear of messing up
God's reason for such
victimizing
flattening
battering

everything does *not* happen
for a reason

        unless one of the reasons
        is randomness
        which by definition
        is something that happens
        without reason

oh, and here's
a head-scratching comment
that people have offered up
more than once
following some
ridiculous event
i've gone through
        God must have big plans for you

sigh, this comment
actually, *all* these comments
reveal something troubling
about God

reveal something troubling
about how our culture
has conditioned
people to think
about God

i mean, i don't really
blame people
for saying these things
i'm sure i have parroted some
anemic platitudes
you know

felt the need to
say something to help
domesticate the unknown

but going through
all this absurdity
has relieved me of
the need

look
if i
had to believe
these events
were manufactured
in the service of some
big plan
God had for me
count me out
i do *not* need a God
like that

idk for sure
but i'm guessing
there's a chance
that if God's involved
with all of this
he or she has resources
slightly more benevolent
slightly more creative
than fires
rapes
and murders

to get me on the
right track

not only does this
not make sense
it's
abhorrent

strange
all the stuff that comes
along with grief

you got your loss and
existential despair
you got to deal with
and then on top of that
you got all the stuff
people say

like, you got
your own problems
and then you got
the problems of others who
cannot bear to
consider the intensity
of your problems
because it
reminds them
of the intensity
of their problems

i don't need to
point my finger at people
for what they say
      though in due time
      i'm more than willing
      to point my finger
      at meaning-making systems

generally responsible
for teaching people
to say such things
but no
i don't need to
blame as much as express
how weird and uncomfortable
it is to find people responding to
massive
gaping-hole
problem
with something
they read on a postcard
once while waiting in line
at a cracker barrel

so what *does* someone say
in these situations?

what *would* be helpful?

i kind of think it's
less about
the right thing to say
and more about
the recognition
nothing said
can make it right

i kind of think it's
less about words
and more about
friendship

friendship
feels like such a
small thing

but like a fulcrum
small things help
move big things

problem is
no one ever says
> *you know what i'd like?*
> *i'd like to be in a relationship with someone*
> *so that when all hell breaks loose*
> *i can be there for them*
> *you know*
> *like a fulcrum*

but if you can be a fulcrum
it might wind up being
a big thing for your friend

in other words
it's no small thing
being a small thing

so if you are sensing
an invitation to be a friend
i'd say go for
solidarity

over
solutions

doesn't mean your friend
won't be searching for solutions
actually, i'm *sure*
they'll be searching for solutions
sometimes in a
paralyzed-deer-in-headlight
kind of way
sometimes in a
paroxysmal-busted-fire-hydrant
kind of way

thing is
your friend's probably not
able to process anything
~~for a couple of days~~
~~for a couple of months~~
for a couple of years

which might mean
your friendship
is the answer

your willingness
not to rush to an answer
is the answer

when someone is
going through hell
you really can't
get em out

drop em a pin
give em a map
throw em a rope
toss em a lifeline

honestly?
you're probably
going to have to go in there
yourself

don't say a bunch of stuff
just go in there
be there

friend is the name
we give to people
who are with us
in hell

solidarity
is commitment
to friendship

it might also be
a commitment
to reality
for to turn your back
on a friend
is to pretend
you are not
interconnected
and separateness is anti-reality

separateness
leads to duplicity
a lack of internal structure
i name as integrity

i leave room to talk about
boundaries
because some things
and some people
must be interacted with carefully
but i think reality is telling us
everything is longing to be
present to everything else

i think this is true
even with hell

i don't think hell is
a destination for
bad people

i doubt
God's interested
in such labels
        good people
        bad people

i think it's a
bit
more nuanced
than that

that hell is
probably something
that's emerged
(and continues to emerge)
out of an
interaction between
overwhelming abundance of
resistance i name as chaos
and our
shame and despair

we can't do much about
overwhelming abundance of
resistance called chaos

but we might be able to do
something about
shame and despair

to not do something
is to be in a type of
solidarity
with chaos
and potentially
create hell

i just don't think
God ever intended
such a place
either in this dimension
or in whatever dimension
comes next

i think hell is a
a space we created
(and continue to create)
out of our misinterpretation
of the chaos

the misinterpretation
led us to consider
the divine as separate
from us

but separateness is anti-reality

and in our confusion
about reality
and anti-reality
scarcity slithered in
and emphasized our
shame and despair

all of it coalesced
(and continues to coalesce)
to create hell

i don't talk this way
to try and diminish
the consequential reality of
such a place
no
i think
hell is a terrible fire that burns

i just think
love is a fire that burns too

maybe hell
is the burning of
love's invitation
to be embraced

if everything is
trying to be present to
everything else
then there is no
love-forsaken space
in the entire cosmos

so hell could be
a burning
and love could be
a deeper burning

maybe hell needs people
with the internal strength
to be in solidarity with its
deeper fire

the deeper fire
isn't some miraculous
touch from the divine
enabling one
to no longer feel pain

the deeper fire
is the invitation
and strength to
hold all the pain
without shame or despair
(no less miraculous)

the pain is
the wrenching between
thing gone and
new things
longing to grow

hell is
death
decay
compost
brilliant
irreparable
resignation
and also
emergence

hell is procreative
hell is living

blessed are those
interested in
living

i think
what i think
is that hell needs a hug

hugs
remind me of
haiti
our girl spent
one short week there
in the remote
mountain area
of the southeast
building a clinic
building friendships
building memories
for a lifetime
(truncated as it was)

sometimes i imagine
what drone footage
of her arrival there
might have been like
    high above
    looking down upon
    matchbox sized
    white suv
    crawling through
    miniature
    forests
    rivers
    villages

    if i allow the eyes
    of my imagination

to go unfocused
the whole scene feels alive
as if the land actively
welcomes her in
slow motion as she moves
up and into
the heart of the island
like a child
falling deeper into the arms
of loving grandparent
    mountains
    giving her
    one
    long
    hug

she came home
from that trip animated
she loved
the adventure
those people
that island
the way it embraced her

she spoke frequently
about returning to haiti
none of us ever imagined
she wouldn't
[ ]

six months after
becoming a fraction
i was trying to

figure out
~~how to do life~~
i was trying to
figure out
life

felt like character
in video game
caught in loop
stuck in corner
of the screen
legs continually
running into a wall
legs continually
running into a wall
legs continually
running into a wall

then wife
boys and i
decided
to go to haiti

maybe we could
get unstuck

maybe we could
help some people
build a soccer field

maybe we could give
haiti a hug
for first hugging our girl

retraced
her trip
up and into
the island
difficult as it was

roads in rural haiti
are less roads and more
dried riverbeds
flowing riverbeds
inclines
cliffsides
culverts
rocks
sand
mud

forehead kept bouncing
off passenger window
soul kept bouncing
off no-thing
shafts of sunlight
filtered through
banana groves
like arpeggiated grief

after several
winding hours
we shot up the last hill
into a splash of sunshine

on top of a little mountain
nestled within a semi-circle
of bigger mountains
all acting like older siblings
squeezing in close
to say hello

it's a stunning place
360 degrees of
waterfalls folded
into valleys folded
into land and sky
stretching out
in one direction
to the very edge
of what you can see
which on a clear day
might be the ocean

i remember the day as
cloudy and humid
it struck me strange
that the clouds didn't
offer relief from the sun
rather
clouds intensified the sun

it struck me strange how
clouds intensified everything

like blankets of depth
on top of more blankets
yeah, like a bunch of

wool blankets
sealing in all the clamminess

we had a meeting
with about twenty
of us in a little clinic
(same clinic our girl
had helped construct
on her trip there)

we wanted a meeting
to make sure the
locals were interested in
a soccer field
to make sure
it wasn't just something
we wanted

like, was this an attempt
to fill the no-thing
inside of us
with another thing?
or was it something
they might find beneficial

turns out
it was a little of both

wife and i sat upfront
facing the locals who
filled in first three rows
leaving back of room
empty

clearly not americans
americans would have
filled in *back* three rows
leaving front of room
empty

haitians sat directly
in front of us
so close
i could've leaned forward
and tapped them
on the forehead, thought
  why are they so close?
  if we were in a boat
  we would capsize
  why …
  why are they so close?

humidity was stifling
sweat rolled down back
jeans clung to legs
claustrophobic
is the
word

there were three
small windows
that were too high to see
outside from my
seated position

but i could hear
kick of

soccer ball
laughter
and chatter of
haitian creole
from local children

it was same location
our girl had played soccer
same local children too
    as the story goes
    (that our daughter
    loved to tell)
    the boys were surprised
    a girl could play so well
    so at end of the week
    they awarded her
    mvp

        i imagined her laughing
        holding hands out to
        calm exaggerated applause
        accepting the honor with
        mock modesty
        as the caribbean sun
        washed all the smiles
        blues to
        yellows to
        white

part of me was
imagining the mvp award
other part of me was
in the little building

under blankets of humidity
pretending
to be happy with
people sitting so close
on front row

as i flickered
back and forth
between
reality and imagination
our haitian friend
introduced us

he talked about
how far we had come
geographically
how much we had been through
emotionally
how much we had given
financially
and the love that had brought us there

except when the words
were translated
in broken english
"love" with a v
came out as "luf" with a f

then it was my turn
to greet the people
to say something
about us
about them

about their community
about the idea of a soccer field
about *anything*
but there
there was just
so much luf

idk
maybe it was
sweat in the eye or
proximity of haitans or
the sounds
coming through
the three little
windows
but i couldn't speak
stuff started glitching

wiped my forehead
as i turned internal
dials and knobs to
focus
but i kept seeing
daughter
in back of room
kept thinking about
how much
pain and gratitude
i had
just kept feeling
so
much
luf

seemed odd
luf wasn't providing
relief from sorrow

rather
luf was intensifying everything
like, blankets of depth
on top of more blankets
sealing the moment
together

i was undone
couldn't speak
thankfully wife was
more than capable

she began
telling the story
asking permission
confirming interest

in time
i lost sense of
time
and
her voice
faded
into the gentle sound
of rain coming through
the three windows
as if the island itself
was crying

heaven
might be
the space
      on the other side
      of windows
      too high to see through
responsible for
the sound that lures
everyone and everything
forward

i don't think heaven
is a destination for
good people

i doubt
God's interested
in such labels
      bad people
      good people

i think it's a
bit
more nuanced
than that

for one thing
humanity
doesn't really have

a shared definition
of good people

for another thing
whatever the
definition
i'm pretty sure
i've got some stuff
that could get me
labeled both
good and
bad

    remember
    watching a movie
    one time with our
    three-year old boy

    beginning of show
    made it obvious who
    the antagonist was

    my boy
    pointed his little finger, declared
        he's the bad guy

    and end of show
    made it obvious
    the antagonist had a
    dramatic
    change of heart

my boy
was very impressed, exclaimed
now he's a good-bad guy

sounds about right

i suspect heaven is
probably something
that's emerged
(and continues to emerge)
out of the willingness of
good-bad guys to
keep listening for
the beauty

sometimes
the resistance is
so overwhelming
that beauty is wrecked
it's terrible and
discordant
    nothing to do
    but bow our head
    at picture window
    and wait

but in the waiting
it's possible
to find inner strength
to bring hope
into the resistance

i think
the sound of heaven
energizes
that kind of inner strength
and that kind of inner strength
energizes
the sound of heaven

beauty is the soundtrack
to heaven's world-making

this could be true
with whatever is
going on there
in that place
but also
here

this could be true
with whatever is
going on
in a later time
but also
now

and honestly
i really don't
think it makes much sense
to talk about what's going
on later
if we're not
talking about what's going
on now

in other words
what we do now
determines the later

i think heaven
is a reality but
to borrow from caputo
it *insists*
more than *exists*
and whether it *exists*
is in part
up to us

i think the same
is true for God
given heaven's
entanglement with God

whether or not
God exists
is in part
up to us

for God cannot
hold the orphan
feed the hungry
sit close to the lonely at
lunchroom table

God cannot
build the levee
insert the needle

sit close to the lonely at
gravesite

but we can

i think God
is a reality but
to borrow from heschel
>   *God's waiting*
>   *to be disclosed*

and in the disclosure
beauty is influenced
and heaven is altered
and our experience is changed
along with our future
which changes God's experience
along with God's future

wait, can God be changed?
i think so for
>   as the baby grows
>   in the womb
>   so the mom grows
>   in her world

i think God
might be a mom

moms
and children
live in great overlap

      the baby's mind develops
      in the womb
      which means
      mom's experience informs
      baby's actual experience

      the mom's body receives
      cells from the baby
      which means
      baby's experience informs
      mom's actual experience

what is true with
mom and baby
is true with all of us
by gradation

our interacting
bodies
lives
dreams
ideas
passions
desires
experiences

environment
constitute each other's existence

    it's a nested system

        one's existence is never
        entirely their own
        we're all in
        a great overlap

it's true that
death is the cessation
of blood pumping
lungs breathing and
brain firing

and if one had
a visual spectrometer kind of thing
like, a visual display measuring
the interaction
bouncing around
within a
family of five doing life
    you know, interacting
    playing
    arguing
    talking
    singing
    taking trips together

and one of the five died?
the display would
grow muted

in certain areas
even dark

however

if it was possible to keep the
visual spectrometer kind of thing
powered on
as they went deep into
the resistance
    grieving
    weeping
    gasping
    screaming
    working
    singing
    praying
    hoping
    dreaming
    hugging
    helping
    building
you know, deep into the resistance
to find beauty and live

in time

the visual spectrometer kind of thing
might begin to
flicker
materialize and
form surprising
new patterns

my little fraction
carries
our girl
in that she is
entrained
embedded
embodied
within us
    cells
    humor
    dreams
    neurons
    memories
    passion
    music
    ideas
    haiti
    love

all of it enlivens us
forward
into the life
of others with whom
we are
entrained
embedded
embodied

and they
the same
for others

multiply this by
billions of people
and billions of trillions
of creatures
in the world
and countless
interactive entities
in the cosmos
and what you have is
an impossible-to-imagine
overlap
        nested systems
        within nested systems
        perishing
        entangling
        enlivening
        constituents of even
        more nested systems

idk anything for sure
but i suspect
all this overlap
might be God

and if God
well …
anything is possible

i'm thoughtful about
such reflections
i'm not trying to
equate possibility
with panacea

and i'm not trying to
diminish pain
for the past
has been a car wreck
of irreversible heartache
> but does the past really have the final say?

    remember hearing
    about my friend adam
    and his friends of
    african descent
    talk about returning to
    their homeland
    of ghana

    they walked
    through
    remnants and
    signs and
    wounds of a land
    destroyed by
    colonial holocaust

    structures
    still exist there
    that were once
    prisons
    these places are called
    slave castles

    adam
    walked through a slave castle
        touched walls

        descended steps
        gripped bars
        and imagined
        what it would
        have been like
        for his ancestors to
        touch
        descend
        and grip

in the back of
these slave castles
are infamous exits
doorways
portals
that were called
the door of no return

the human beings
kidnapped
chained and shoved
through the door
knew exactly
what it meant
    their home
    family
    culture
    identity
    gone forever

it was
the door of no return
and yet

adam
and his friends of
african descent
did return
intentionally
defiantly
freely
to grieve the past
to consider possibilities
for the future

i'm thoughtful about
such reflections
i'm not trying to
equate possibility
with panacea

and i'm not trying to
diminish pain
for the past
has been a genocide
of irreversible heartache
 but does the past really have the final say?

grieving
is a slow arrow

a renegotiation with time
to live best one can
without thinking
too far ahead
      the next milestones
      like millstones
      around the neck of our future
           birthdays
           holidays
           anniversaries

it's a commitment
to each day
full of grace
by the hour

grieving
is redirection of power
to give one's
impatience a hug
to be powerful
in powerless waiting

grieving
is redefinition of attachment
to let go of letting go
to see oneself attached

to the absence
that does not let go

    remember
    random hug
    our girl gave
    a few months
    before
    death

    she was
    a busy nursing student
        papers to write
        people to talk to
        places to go

    but as she clipped
    through the kitchen
    one day
    she took a detour
    found me and
    gave a random hug

    i wrapped arms around her
    and felt the puffiness
    of her winter coat deflate
    in rhythm to her exhale

        she sank into the embrace
        rested for a moment, said
            you smell like daddy

    didn't ask her
    what that meant
    but i imagined part
    fragrance part
    strength part
    home

and now?
i'm permanently
attached to
the existence
of non-existent
random kitchen hugs
i hate it and i accept it
there's a certain kind of sweetness here
    i imagine part
    fragrance part
    strength part
    home
    (the longing of)

grieving
is the longing
for home

home
can happen in a house
but a house
isn't necessarily a home

house is way things are formed
home is way things function

houses play a role
but the point
is the home

i'd rather live
with love
in the poorhouse
than without love
in a penthouse

what I'm
trying to say is
love doesn't force stuff
    matter
    relationships
    theology
    morality
to go one particular way
    pre-determined
    set in stone
    for all time

no
love's infused within
all things
working
inviting
consenting
unleashing
endlessly creative

love is possibility
even amid the chaos

love is the design

home
isn't what i
thought it once was
but then again … *what is?*

everything is changing

if it's about form
then i'm doomed
but if it's about function
there's a chance
things could get re
worked re
imagined re
created

but i have to be honest
there's also a chance
it could go poorly

all we really have
is faith

faith comes by
      hearing
hearing comes by
      word of God
word of God comes by
      conviction
      whispers
      hints
      text
      courage
      intuitions
      admonition
      commitment
      songs
      impressions

            had a dream once
            was in a large
            dark and spacious house
            way out in a forest
            when suddenly
            i became aware of music

            not that the music was
            suddenly loud
            just that i had the sudden
            awareness of music
            in the background

i got up to find
where the soundtrack
was coming from
you know, mobile device or
record player or
stereo

i searched room to room
top
to
bottom
but couldn't locate
the source

it wasn't a scary dream
wasn't a nightmare
it was just odd

completely dark
no charging devices
no blinking screens
no moonlight or stars

i was in a big dark house
in the middle of nowhere
without any source of energy
and as i awakened i thought
  weird
   there's no power and yet there's music

i think what i think is
as absurd as my loss is

it doesn't exist in
isolation

my no-thing is connected
to some-thing
and that some-thing
just might be love

i might be wrong
because
most of the time
it's dark and there's
no power

        then again
            where's that music coming from?

and
now these two questions remain
> *why do bad things happen?*
> *and why do good things happen?*

but the greatest of these is
> *why do good things happen?*

epilogue

present
throbs of beauty
the past electricity

lingers
in the air
power etched
in an outline
flash
across the backdrop
of all we see
the detonation is brilliant
lightning bolt

beauty terrible beauty
air charged with a buzz
pine trees in sway
atmosphere smell
i remember

underneath
root and rock
with father
below the tree line
ducking

plastic-hooded raincoats
amplified the
dramatic raindrops
rocky mountain explosions

on top of us
behind us
before us
shale and rock

the mountainside
scrambling up toward
brooding skies

> *thunder*

endnotes

absence

The theme of no-thing as a some-thing has been on my mind for a couple of years, so I was energized and more than intrigued to read some of Richard Boothby's slant on the idea in his insightful book *Blown Away: Refinding Life after My Son's Suicide*, Other Press. 2022. Boothby explores this idea more in his subsequent book *Embracing the Void: Rethinking the Origin of the Sacred*, Northwestern University Press. 2022.

early

Elie Wiesel's story about the concentration camp march takes place in *Night*. Hill and Wang; 2nd edition translated by Marion Weisel. 2012, Kindle Edition, loc. 1035. A side note to this endnote is that this edition, translated by Elie's wife, Marion, is my *Night* of choice. The preface contains some excerpts that, as absurd as it seems now, were cut from the original manuscript.

midday

The Mark Twain quote comes from some reflections published posthumously. *A Family Sketch and Other Private Writings (Jumping Frogs: Undiscovered, Rediscovered, and Celebrated Writings of Mark Twain Book 5)*, University of California Press; 1st edition. 2014, p. 13.

she's

The film quote comes from *Wind River*, directed by Taylor Sheridan (2017 - https://www.imdb.com/title/tt5362988/?ref_=tt_mv_close)

followed

Regarding organ donations, we were honored to work with the Midwest Transplant Network https://mwtn.org.

strange

The line about "the intensity of other people's problems" is adapted from some writing by Cheryl Strayed, the author of *Tiny Beautiful Things: Advice from Dear Sugar,* VINTAGE BOOKS EDITIONS. 2022.

solidarity

"Love flashes like fire, the brightest kind of flame" is found in Song of Solomon 8:6 https://www.biblegateway.com/passage/?search=Song+of+Solomon+8%3A6&version=NLT

retraced

You're invited to check www.lovehaitit.org for more info about what we do in Haiti.

heaven

John Caputo's famous line can be found in the first paragraph of the preface of *The Insistence of God: A Theology of Perhaps (Indiana Series in the Philosophy of Religion)*, Indiana University Press, 2013.

endnotes

Abraham Joshua Heschel's line in *The Sabbath* is, "Yet those who realize that God is at least as great as the known universe, that the spirit is an endless process of which we humbly partake, will understand and experience what it means that *the spirit is disclosed at certain moments of time*." *The Sabbath: It's Meaning for Modern Man (FSG Classics)*. Farrar, Straus and Giroux. 1951. Kindle Edition, p. 78.

moms

Alfred North Whitehead describes a "fluency whereby the perishing of the process, on the completion of the particular existent, constitutes that existent as an original element in the constitutions of other particular existents elicited by repetitions of process." Something he called "transition." *Process and Reality*, Edited by Griffin and Sherburn. The Free Press. 1978. Kindle edition, p. 210.

My friend Charles Bakker emailed me on June 24, 2023, and said, "Since we are all processes, and since we all entrain each other's processes in different ways, then there are aspects of your process which are quite literally the continuing of processes which only your loved one could have entrained you into engaging in. Insofar, then, as you continue as a process, your loved one partially continues on as a process in you. Yes, you lose them in part, just as you lose a part of yourself. But you cannot lose them totally, unless you, too, are lost totally."

The slave castle story comes from Adam Clark in an email to me on June 27, 2023, but also on Tripp Fuller's "Homebrewed podcast episode - Adam Clark: From Contemplation to Liberation," which was posted June 20, 2023. https://podcasts.apple.com/us/podcast/homebrewed-christianity-podcast/id276269040?i=1000617751549

grieving

"Grieving is a slow arrow" is a line borrowed (and adapted) from Nietzsche, who said, "Beauty is a slow arrow." Strangely, I cannot find the quote in my edition of Nietzsche's *Human, All-Too-Human*, but I have seen others quote it in the version translated by Marion Faber (London: Penguin, 1994), p. 104. (And speaking of Byung-Chul Han, much of what I said about beauty resonates with his writing. Then again, much of it resonates with Catherine Keller, Peter Rollins, John O'Donahue, Hegel, Whitehead, and others.)

acknowledgments

i acknowledge none of this would have been written without johnna, and the boys, and the girls the boys have brought into our life (her sisters-in-love), and nephews and nieces (her cousins), and siblings (her aunts and uncles), and moms and dads (her grandparents), and friends that flew across the country, and julie, my editor, who's not really *my* editor but you know what i mean, and phoenix the dog, and our faith community when all this went down—how they packed out the house night after night for several days, food like little hills of affection piled up around the kitchen, appendages of young people sprawled across the living room floor like threads of fabric holding us together, singing songs with our boys …

i also acknowledge mountains, and forests, and prayer, and music, and beauty, and love, and hope that comes in all shapes and sizes depending on one's experience and tradition, my tradition being one that is super interested in the way a young hebrew man lived a couple of thousand years ago, and lots and lots of authors, and humanity, because none of this happens in a vacuum, everything is connected to everything else …

yeah, sounds about right

about the author

Jonathan is the husband of one and father of three, has degrees from NorthWind Seminary, is an author, podcaster, former church planter, and spends a lot of time thinking about lovehaiti.org. Find out more at jonathanfosteronline.com.

other writing

https://fosterj.substack.com

Theology of Consent: Mimetic Theory in an Open and Relational Universe

The Reconstructionist: People>Text, Mercy>Sacrifice, Love>Fear

Questions About Sexuality that Got me Uninvited from My Denomination

Made in the USA
Thornton, CO
04/01/24 10:11:57

6321cf42-5a79-447b-9e68-3abf1e3514baR01